Julia Ferenc

creating SILVER JEWELRY with BEADS

**LITTLE
CRAFT BOOK
SERIES**

By Marianne Seitz

STERLING
PUBLISHING CO., INC. NEW YORK
SAUNDERS OF TORONTO, Ltd., Don Mills, Canada

Oak Tree Press Co., Ltd.
London & Sydney

Little Craft Book Series

Bargello Stitchery
Beads Plus Macramé
Big-Knot Macramé
Candle-Making
Cellophane Creations
Coloring Papers
Corrugated Carton Crafting
Creating Silver Jewelry with Beads
Creating with Beads
Creating with Burlap
Creating with Flexible Foam
Enamel without Heat
Felt Crafting
Flower Pressing
Ideas for Collage
Lacquer and Crackle

Macramé
Making Paper Flowers
Making Shell Flowers
Masks
Metal and Wire Sculpture
Model Boat Building
Nail Sculpture
Needlepoint Simplified
Off-Loom Weaving
Potato Printing
Puppet-Making
Repoussage
Scissorscraft
Scrimshaw
Sewing without a Pattern
Tole Painting

Whittling and Wood Carving

The original edition was published in West Germany under the title "Schmuck aus Perlen Draht und Silberblech" © 1971 by Don Bosco Verlag, Munich, Germany.

Translated by Manly Banister
Adapted by Anne E. Kallem

Contents

Before You Begin 5
   Materials . . . Tools
A Looped-Wire and Bead Necklace 9
A Looped-Wire and Bead Bracelet 11
Neckloop with Pendant and Matching Earrings 12
A Wire Neckloop and Jewelled Silver Pendant 14
A Neckloop with a Flat-Wire and Cameo Pendant 16
A Flat-Wire Neckloop with Spiral and Bead Pendant 17
Twisted Wire Neckloop with Spiral and Bead Pendant 20
A Linked Wire and Bead Belt 21
Spiralled Flat-Wire and Bead Choker 22
Silver-and-Bead-Decorated Velvet Chokers 23
Silver Gorget and Matching Earrings 27
A Personalized Silver and Bead Barrette 30
Spiralled Flat-Wire Belt and Armband 31
A Beaded Wire Necklace and Bracelet 32
Neckpiece and Cuff Links 37
Wire-and-Bead-Decorated Belt 38
Hammered Silver Round-Wire Hairpin 39
A Flat-Wire Key Ring 40
Round-Wire-and-Bead Key Ring Pendant 41
Spiralled Round-Wire Bottle Collar 42
A Round-Wire Wall Decoration 43
A Wire-and-Bead Christmas Decoration 47
Index 48

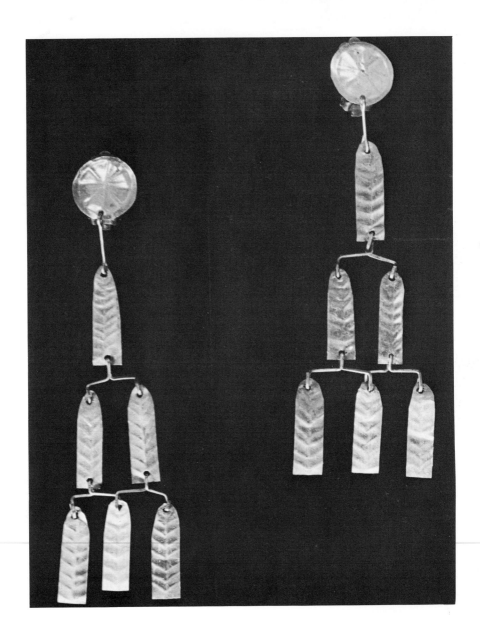

Before You Begin

Silver, besides being one of the most attractive of Nature's metals, is also one of the most malleable, or softest, of all metals, natural or man-made. In addition, it is far less expensive than, say, gold. Besides the satisfaction you will find in your completed silver jewelry, you will discover the joy of working with this lovely metal. It has a texture and other qualities that are far different from ordinary metals.

You are going to be amazed at the ease with which you can produce stunning, individual jewelry—*without any difficult techniques,* such as sawing, drilling, or soldering. With your own two hands and a minimum of materials and tools, you can turn out in combination with beads the most intricate, finely wrought silver jewelry imaginable.

A word of caution. Before you begin any project, read the instructions carefully first, so you have a clear idea of what you are going to do. Assemble *all* of your materials and tools so you won't be left hanging in mid-air, both hands occupied, and minus a vital piece of wire.

Finally, do not be deceived by the elaborate appearance of some of the projects in this book. Every piece is as simple as the few techniques you will learn right in the beginning!

Materials

The first thing you will need of course, is silver wire and sheet silver. You will use *wire* in almost all of your projects. There are many different sizes and shapes available which you can purchase from a metal supply house, as well as through specialized hobby shops. You will find round, flat, rectangular, square, beaded, half-round, etc. However, for your beginning work in this book, you will use only round and flat.

Wire thickness is expressed in terms of gauge: 1 gauge is equivalent to 7.341 mm. or 0.289 in. The higher the gauge number, the finer the wire; that is, a 10-gauge wire is heavier, or thicker, than a 20-gauge wire. Round wire (see Illus. 1) is difficult to work with in the heavier gauges, so keep to the 16- to 24-gauge area. Silver flat wire comes in various widths, but you will find the $\frac{1}{8}$"-width suitable for your jewelry. A piece of 18-gauge flat wire can be hammered out to make it wider if so desired (see Illus. 1).

You will generally want to use the higher gauge (lightweight) wires which, incidentally, are the least expensive. Silver is sold by weight and therefore the lower gauge, or thicker, wires are heavier and cost more. Also, the thinner the silver, the more malleable it is.

The same holds true for *sheet silver.* This you

WIRE

Round

B & S Gauge

B & S Gauge	
9	●
12	●
16	●
18	•
20	•
24	•

Illus. 1. These are some of the wire and sheet-metal gauges you will find available. The thicknesses shown are actual size.

Flat

— 18 B & S (10 gauges hard)

SHEET

B & S Gauge

B & S Gauge	
12	▬▬▬▬▬▬▬
14	▬▬▬▬▬▬▬
16	▬▬▬▬▬▬▬
18	▬▬▬▬▬▬▬
20	▬▬▬▬▬▬▬
22	▬▬▬▬▬▬▬
24	▬▬▬▬▬▬▬
26	▬▬▬▬▬▬▬

will find available in a variety of sizes and shapes—strips, circles, squares, and so on, in gauges from 10 to 28. You will, of course, as with the wire, want to use the lighter-weight pieces, say from 18 gauge up. As you can see from Illus. 1, 12 gauge would be entirely too thick for your purposes. It is advisable to use none heavier than 24 gauge, and preferably 28 gauge.

Beads you can choose at your whim. No doubt you have a collection already of broken or unused necklaces, bracelets, earrings, even beadlike buttons. If not, you can easily find glass, plastic, wooden, or enamel beads at variety shops. Do be sure to get an assortment that have varying sizes of "eyes" to adjust to the width of the wires you will be using.

Findings are ready-made devices to use as backings for many of your finished pieces. You need not use silver unless you wish to—you can purchase very inexpensive metal findings in a hobby or variety shop. However, in much of your silverwork you are going to make your own clasps and such, but for earrings, you will probably want ready-made findings.

Tools

A very simple assortment of tools are needed—some of which you will have on hand already. *Round-nose pliers* (see Illus. 32) are used to bend and shape both round and flat wire, as well as for gripping, in the same way a tweezers is used. They have two round jaws that taper to points. Generally, you will use the round-nose pliers for making rounded forms.

Flat-nose pliers have flat jaws and are used for

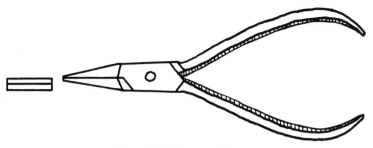

Illus. 2. Flat-nose pliers.

squeezing materials together and for shaping such things as square or angled windings, as well as for straightening out warped pieces. Avoid the pliers that have serrated jaws, or if they do, file them down smooth to keep them from damaging the metal (see Illus. 2).

Diagonal-cutting pliers, also called diagonal wire cutters, have a cutting jaw at an angle up to the point. Use them for cutting off both round and flat wire. There is a type that has a cutter on one jaw in combination with a round or flat jaw. These are less suitable for getting into tight places where it is necessary to snip off wire ends.

Metal-cutting shears, called plate shears (Illus. 32), are necessary only for cutting thicker metals such as earring findings. A simple very sharp scissors is sufficient for your sheet silver cutting.

A rawhide or rubber mallet and a small anvil are handy for hammering and flattening. These are inexpensive and worth the small investment. For wire-bending aids, you can use almost anything that is the right size and shape—a knitting needle, pencil, or yardstick, a bottle, etc. A bone folder is all that is necessary for embossing sheet silver. And finally, epoxy cement for glueing beads onto the metal.

Illus. 3. Diagonal-cutting pliers.

Illus. 4. One piece of wire and some beads and you have a stunning necklace or bracelet. (See page 11 for making the bracelet.)

A Looped-Wire and Bead Necklace

Materials

    18- or 20-gauge silver round wire
    20 beads, 12 light and 8 dark
    round-nose pliers
    diagonal-cutting pliers
    string
    tape measure or yardstick

The necklace in Illus. 4 is so easy to make from just one piece of silver wire, you might end up making dozens of them for friends and relatives.

Take a very long piece of string and place it around your neck. Decide what length you wish the large neckloop to be, remove the string and measure the length. An average size is 15".

Now using the string again, follow Illus. 5 through Illus. 9 until you have formed the three small loops and the neckloop, allowing at least $1\frac{1}{2}''$ for clasping purposes. Undo your "string necklace" and measure the total length. It will probably be about 40" long.

Now you are ready to work with your silver wire and beads. Cut a piece of wire at least 6" longer than you need to allow for adjustments. You are not wasting wire—you will use many small pieces in your work.

With your hands, bend the wire in the middle into the shape shown in Illus. 5. Slide two dark-colored beads on as shown. Then bend wire strand 1 and strand 2 together and thread two more dark beads on both wires. Now bend strand 1 over strand 2 and work the beads gradually downwards to the point where you want your first loop (Illus. 6).

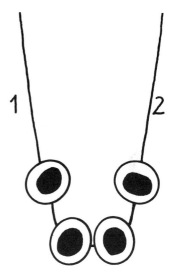

Illus. 5.

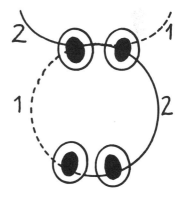

Illus. 6.

9

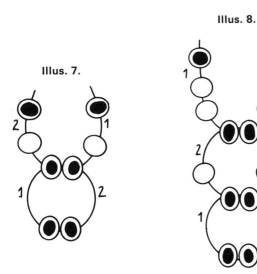

Illus. 7.

Illus. 8.

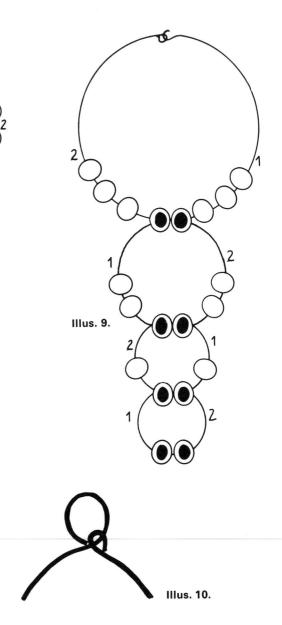

Illus. 9.

Thread two light-colored beads onto the two strands just as you did before by pressing the upper ends together. Work these down in the same way to the point where you want loop #2 (Illus. 7). Thread two more dark beads on, cross the strands over again, and thread four light-colored beads on, two on each side, and complete loop #3 by threading on two more dark beads (Illus. 8).

Add the six light beads shown, three on each side, and bend your two strands into the neckloop shape. Make a simple clasp at the end as shown in Illus. 10. Use the round-nose pliers for this bending procedure. Snip off any excess wire with your diagonal-cutting pliers.

Illus. 10.

10

A Looped-Wire and Bead Bracelet

Materials
  20-gauge silver round wire
  14 beads
  round-nose pliers
  diagonal-cutting pliers
  rolling pin
  string
  cellophane tape
  tape measure or yardstick

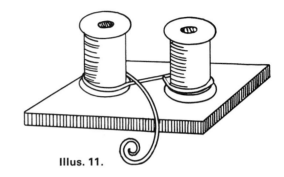

Although our bracelet in Illus. 4 has 24 beads and 12 loops, be a little less ambitious for your first wire and bead bracelet, or you will have to make loops that are too small to handle at this point. Be satisfied with 8 loops and 14 beads. Do not use more than two beads per "twist" unless they are very small.

Take your string and form 8 overlapping loops all stretched out in a line. Use tape to hold the loops together. Pick it up carefully and place it around your wrist. Adjust the loops as necessary—smaller or larger in order to fit. Take note of the two ends, undo the string and measure. An average length is 24″. Again, as you did with your necklace, allow a little extra for clasping.

You can now thread your beads onto the wire in the same way as with the necklace, crossing and threading two beads at a time. For this project, you will find your round-nose pliers most helpful to aid you with the bending. Actually, you can make a very simple device to help in your round bending if you wish, as shown in Illus. 11. This will help you whenever you want to make uniform rounded shapes.

Take two wooden spools of the desired size and nail them down with small nails onto a hard surface. Then bend the wire around the spools as shown, being sure each set of beads is in place as you work each loop.

Now, since your bracelet is still flat, in order to form it into wrist shape, use a wooden or plastic rolling pin to form it on. Work carefully, using your pliers and hands, until the desired shape is attained. For your bracelet, it is best to use the clasp shown in Illus. 12. Shape as shown.

Illus. 12.

Neckloop with Pendant and Matching Earrings

Materials

    silver round wire, 12-gauge most desirable,
      16-gauge satisfactory
    silver flat wire
    beads
    sheet silver, 26 gauge
    silver round wire, 24 gauge
    strong needle
    sharp scissors
    round-nose pliers
    paper
    knitting needle
    spring-type earring findings
    epoxy cement

Using the string method, measure off a piece of 12- or 16-gauge round wire the desired length for the large neck loop. Bend the ends into a hook catch as shown in Illus. 13.

To make the pendant, take a piece of flat wire long enough to accommodate 5 or 6 beads, plus allowance for bending the end around the neck-loop at the top, and at the bottom for hooking on the square. (Remember, it is always wise to use string for your preliminary measurements.)

Do not cut out your sheet-silver square until you have made a paper pattern. This way you can change its size at will—once you cut the sheet-silver square, you can do nothing but make it smaller! Place the pattern on the corner of a silver sheet so you will have two straight edges already cut for you. With a grease pencil, sketch in the other two sides and cut, using sharp scissors. Then with a strong needle, pierce one corner so you have a hole that will accommodate 24-gauge wire.

Now make tiny 24-gauge loops (called "jump rings" in case you wish to purchase them) by winding a length of wire around a knitting needle. You will need 6 for this project, but you can make a number of them at this time for use later. Remove the "spiral" from the needle and cut across one side as shown in Illus. 14, using the diagonal-cutting pliers. Attach two rings to the square, closing both tightly. This you can do by squeezing with your fingers.

Now bend the flat-wire strip around the neckloop using round-nose pliers. String your beads on. Bend the bottom end of the flat wire up and hook the second ring onto it. Bend shut with the pliers.

Make the matching earrings in the same way as you did the pendant. You will undoubtedly use fewer beads and smaller squares, however. With epoxy cement, attach ready-made ear clips to the top end of the flat wire. If they overlap on the side, use your metal-cutting shears to trim them down *before you glue,* or else glue strips of sheet silver the equivalent width of the findings over the flat wire. (If you ever do make a mistake in glueing or decide you want to make a change, there is an epoxy cement remover available.)

Illus. 13.

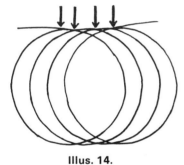

Illus. 14.

Illus. 15. This beautiful silver round-wire neckpiece and matching earrings would do credit to a professional silversmith!

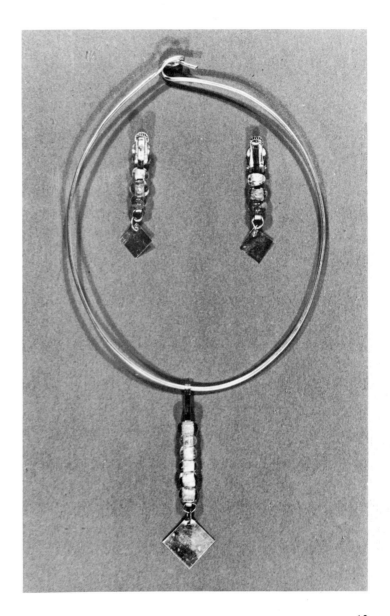

A Wire Neckloop and Jewelled Silver Pendant

Materials

18-gauge silver round wire or lighter
24-gauge silver round wire
sheet silver 26 gauge or lighter
a square bead, not too small
string
strong needle
bone folder
epoxy cement

This is neckloop (1) in Illus. 17.

You will want to use a lightweight wire for this project because the necklace should have a very delicate appearance. If you wish, use a lighter wire than 18 gauge.

Since this type of necklace looks best as a choker, measure off your neck length with your string and cut a corresponding piece of silver round wire. An average length is 15″ or 16″. The loop should be as close to a circle as possible, so shape your wire very carefully, holding one end with the flat-nose pliers and the other with the round-nose pliers. To achieve the best results, you might shape it around a half-gallon or gallon bottle, such as is used for mineral water or wine. Be sure you fill the bottle with liquid so it won't tip during the bending process, or enlist the aid of a friend to hold it steady. Make a simple clasp as in Illus. 13.

Next, make your paper patterns for the square silver pendant and long triangular pieces attached to it. Make these fairly good-sized, say a 2″ square and 2″-long triangles. When you are satisfied with the proportions, outline the patterns on the sheet silver and cut. Pierce the square with a strong needle in three places as shown in Illus. 17. Pierce the triangles at the narrow ends.

Now you can try your hand at some simple embossing. When embossing, you work both sides of the silver, using a bone folder or wooden modelling tool (Illus. 16). If neither is handy, you no doubt have a nonmetallic letter opener which would do as well. Do your embossing on a support such as a hard rubber mat or thick felt mat. (A triple thickness of blotters will also serve the purpose.)

Illus. 16. A typical wooden modelling tool.

Using a grease pencil, sketch in a line all around the square. Our silver square has bevelled edges, achieved by simply cutting off the corners. However, for your first try at embossing, leave it

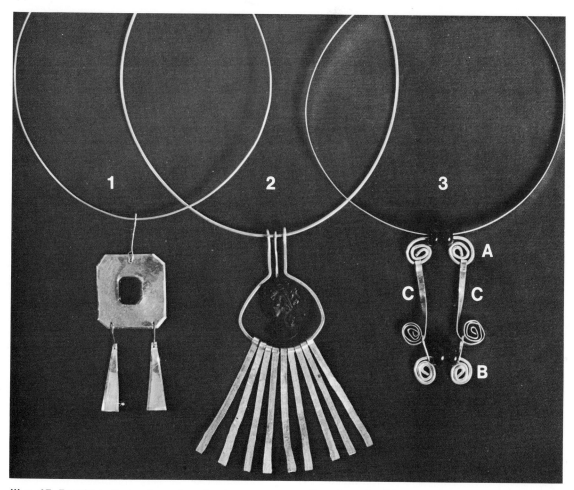

Illus. 17. For these three elegant neck adornments, see directions for (1) on opposite page; (2) on page 16; and (3) on page 17.

Illus. 18. Embossing.

A Neckloop with a

Flat-Wire and

Cameo Pendant

square. Then with your tool, define the line on one side and then on the other as shown in Illus. 18. You may have to work both sides several times to achieve the desired result. Do the same with the triangles, remembering always to emboss on your mat. Do not press hard—a little experimental light pressure is advisable to start.

When you have finished the embossing, cut 1"-long pieces of the 24-gauge silver round wire and make the attachment pieces for the square and

Materials
    18-gauge silver round wire
    18-gauge silver flat wire $\frac{1}{8}$" wide
    large decorative bead, or cameo as shown
    rawhide or rubber mallet (in a pinch you can
       wrap felt around an ordinary hammer)
    anvil
    epoxy cement

Illus. 19. A: Wrong. B: Right.

triangles. Bend these in the fashion shown in Illus. 19 which shows the right way and the wrong way to make this type of attachment loop. Before closing them over completely, insert the ends in the holes you pierced, as well as around the neckloop.

You are now ready to attach the decorative bead in the middle by simply glueing it on with epoxy cement, and you are finished!

This is neckloop (2) in Illus. 17.

Make a choker-type neckloop as you did on page 12.

To decide on the size of the wire which will enclose the cameo, use the string method as before—it should require approximately 10" allowing for the two lengths attached to the neckloop. Use the silver round wire for this part and lay it on the anvil. With the mallet, tap *lightly* along its length until it has two flattened surfaces. Do not flatten it out completely. You will find it has stretched out somewhat. (A tip on hammering: excessive hammering will toughen the metal, so keep this in mind when you work.)

16

In order to bend this wire into the shape shown, you can use any form you might have handy that is similar or you can make a form yourself very easily. Take a block of wood, and hammer nails into your desired pattern as shown in Illus. 20. Then bend the wire around the nails until it has the shape you want. Be sure to snip the heads off the nails so that you can lift the wire off easily.

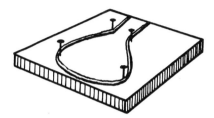

Illus. 20. Shaping wire.

Before attaching this to the neckloop, make your flat-wire strands. Prior to cutting the individual pieces, decide how long they are to be. Since they will be attached to a curved surface, make them all the same length, and they will appear to form a similar curve (see Illus. 17). Suppose you choose 2″ for the length and 9 strands altogether, simply multiply, and cut an 18″-length of flat wire. Hammer this out as much as you please on your anvil. Then measure off each 2″ length and cut. Attach them by bending the ends over the finished part of the pendant and squeezing. Then attach the entire piece to the neckloop with simple bends as shown.

The large bead or cameo is hooked onto the neckloop with a piece of flattened round wire which, in turn, is glued onto the back of the cameo.

A Flat-Wire Neckloop with Spiral and Bead Pendant

Materials
   18-gauge silver flat wire
   18-gauge silver round wire
   24-gauge silver round wire
   4 large-eyed beads
   very narrow string
   round-nose pliers
   flat-nose pliers

This is neckloop (3) in Illus. 17.

Form a choker-type neckloop as before, this time using the 18-gauge flat wire. Do not fashion a clasp immediately—leave the ends free until later on.

The three spiralled parts A, B, and C will be made separately and put together. A and B are made of round wire and C of flat wire.

17

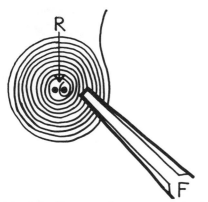

Illus. 21. Spiralling requires use of both the round-nose pliers (R) and the flat-nose pliers (F).

Take your narrow string and make a form with spiralled ends as shown at A in Illus. 17 in proportion to the neckloop. Unravel and measure. Piece B will be similar but somewhat smaller; however, allow the same length for each. You can make tighter spirals for Part B, if you wish. Jot down the measurement, so you won't forget.

Two identical pieces of flat wire comprise Part C. Use a piece of string again to determine how long you want these pieces and make a note of it. They should be the same length, of course, or Part B will hang lopsided.

Cut your first piece of round wire. Then, with your round-nose pliers, grip one end, and with the aid of the flat-nose pliers, wrap a spiral around at least two times (Illus. 21). Now slip two beads on from the other end and proceed to wrap another, similar, spiral at that end. Don't worry if they are not exactly alike—the distinction of hand-made jewelry is that it is rarely precision-wrought!

Make Part C in exactly the same way, forming somewhat tighter spirals and also adding two beads as shown.

Now cut your two pieces for Part C from the flat wire. Make your spirals as before and then, as in Illus. 22, using the round-nose pliers (R), twist the flat wire around the flat-nose pliers (F) a *quarter-turn* (90°) as shown.

You are now ready to attach the various pieces together. Take Part A and thread it onto the neckloop through the eyes of the beads until it is in the exact middle. Join Part C to Part A by inserting the two ends into the lower spirals and bending them over on the reverse side into hooks. Part B and Part C are joined together with the same 24-gauge wire loops which you used on page 16.

Make a clasp on the neckloop and wear your new creation with pride.

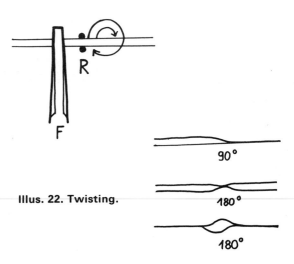

Illus. 22. Twisting.

90°

180°

180°

Illus. 23.

Now that you know how to form
links, how to spiral, and how to
twist, try your hand at the simple
pendant (Illus. 23) and necklace
(Illus. 24).

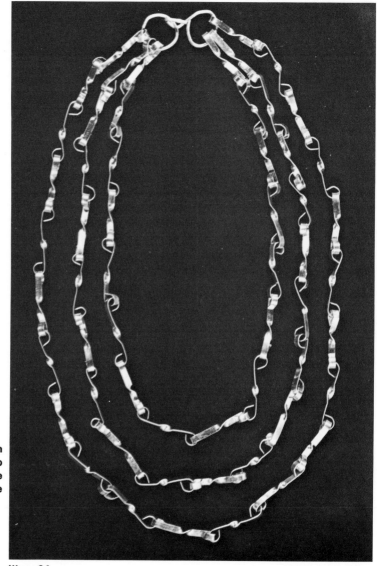

Illus. 24.

Twisted Wire Neckloop with Spiral and Bead Pendant

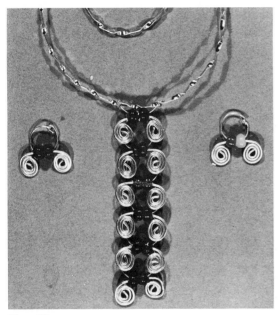

Illus. 25.

Materials
   18-gauge silver flat wire
   20-gauge silver round wire
   24-gauge silver round wire
   12 beads with large eyes
   round-nose pliers
   flat-nose pliers

This elaborate-looking necklace is simpler than you think—it merely combines techniques you have already learned—threading, twisting and spiralling. Each part is made separately and then joined together.

Since you will lose some length in your neckloop because of the twists, allow at least 3″ more when you take your string measurement. You can always snip off any leftover wire, but you cannot add any!

Now, with your round-nose pliers, twist the flat wire around the flat-nose pliers a *half-turn* (180°) as shown in Illus. 22. Continue this process until your neckloop is complete. A simple way to measure off each section between twists is to use the width of the flat-nose pliers as a guide. As we said before, don't be worried if it doesn't come out looking absolutely perfect. That would be impossible even for the most skilled silverworker without the aid of machines which, after all, have no place in our hand-wrought work.

Since all of the spiralled parts are made separately and are all the same size, measure once only with your string as you did on page 18. You will make six of these parts, but cut just one piece first from your 18-gauge round wire to make sure it is correct. Then proceed to spiral one end, slip on two beads and spiral the other end, exactly as you did for Parts A and B in Illus. 17. Continue until you have made all six pieces.

Take your 24-gauge wire, and proceed to "thread" it through each pair of beads as you did for your first necklace on page 9. Attach the two strands to your neckloop with a few twists. Snip off any loose ends, and make a neckclasp as shown in Illus. 10.

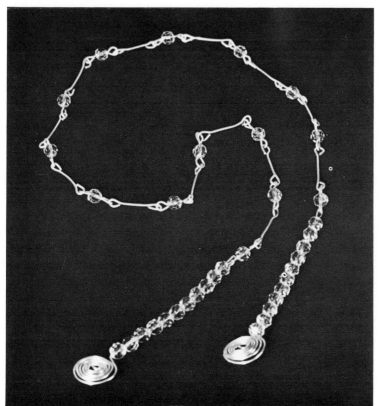

A Linked Wire and Bead Belt

Illus. 26.

Materials

24-gauge silver round wire

quantity of glass or plastic beads with small eyes

round-nose pliers

flat-nose pliers

The individual links of this delicate-looking belt are made in two different lengths. Make a string measurement of your waist. The number of beads and links will depend upon how long your belt will be. Our belt is based upon a 28″ or 30″ waist. We have used fourteen 1″ links and fourteen $\frac{1}{2}$″ links which add up to 21″.

Then we have used about 6″ of round wire on each end to string two rows of beads. However, our belt has spirals on the ends which not only serve to hold the beads, but can be used as a clasp by simply hooking them one over the other.

Make your links in the same way as you made

21

the connecting links in Illus. 19. Every other link will be a short one on which you will thread one bead before closing the ends. Be sure to hook each link onto the next one before closing tightly. Actually, it is wise not to squeeze them tight until you have completed all the links in case you want to make an adjustment.

For the two end pieces which are hooked onto the last links, use about 16″ of round wire for each. Make your spirals using the pliers. String the beads on. Snip the leftovers, if any, leaving $\frac{3}{4}$″ for a hook.

You can make all kinds of variations of this belt, or you might wish to make a matching bracelet or earrings.

Spiralled Flat-Wire and Bead Choker

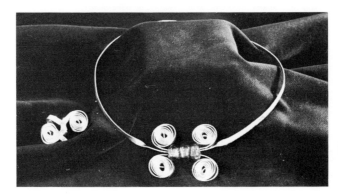

Illus. 27.

Materials
18-gauge silver flat wire $\frac{1}{8}$″ wide
24-gauge silver flat wire
3 beads with extra large eyes
round-nose and flat-nose pliers

Make your choker from the 18-gauge flat wire, allowing a little for two twists. Do not make the clasp until later.

Cut two 16″-pieces of 24-gauge flat wire. Form spirals with your pliers on *one* end of each. Pass the free ends of both through the three beads so they are in the relative positions shown in the photograph. Then spiral the other two ends.

Slip the choker through the beads and *between* the other two pieces of wire. Then, with the pliers twist the flat wire a quarter-turn (90°). Make a clasp with the ends and you're finished.

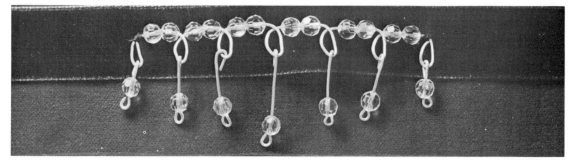

Silver-and-Bead-Decorated Velvet Chokers

Materials

For the choker in Illus. 28, you will need:
  velvet neckband available in variety stores
  24-gauge, or lighter, silver round wire
  19 small beads with small eyes
  round-nose pliers
  knitting needle
  needle and thread

For the choker in Illus. 29, you will need:
  26-gauge sheet silver
  large jewel-like bead
  24-gauge, or lighter, silver round wire
  strong needle
  sharp scissors
  bone folder
  mat for embossing
  epoxy cement

Illus. 29.

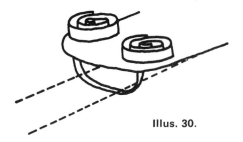

Illus. 30.

The unusual wire and bead decoration in Illus. 28 is approximately 6″ long. Cut a 10″ length of the wire. Starting on the left for ease in working (or on the right if you are left-handed), use your pliers and knitting needle to form a small, long loop about 1″ long. Slip on two beads from the other end and form another loop. Slip on two more beads and continue in this way until you have made seven loops, using twelve beads.

Next, make seven links as shown, in four lengths—cut two at a time for the six links on either side of the middle, longest, one. After making the loop on each link the "right way" shown in Illus. 19, slip on a bead and form half-closed attachments on the other ends. Place these, one at a time, on the main piece as shown, and close tight.

With heavy thread, sew the two ends onto the velvet ribbon, using thread the same color as the velvet.

The necklace on the back cover of this book was made using this same basic procedure.

The embossed sheet silver decoration in Illus. 29 is easily adapted to a belt or brooch as well as the choker.

Make your paper pattern for the shape you choose, outline it with a grease pencil on the silver, and then cut. A good size for this ornament is $2\frac{1}{2}″ \times 1\frac{1}{2}″$. Before you begin embossing, pierce four holes, two at each end, about $\frac{1}{2}″$ in from the ends. The two holes on either end should be as far away from each other as the width of the velvet. Emboss your design within the area between the holes. Then poke the two ends of a piece of fine round wire through each end pair of holes from back to front, and wind the ends into spirals. On the back of the wires, you will have formed loops similar to belt loops through which you insert the velvet ribbon (see Illus. 30).

Lastly, cement the large bead in the middle of the decoration.

Illus. 31.

Illus. 32. Silver wire, silver sheet and beads are all that are required to turn out the handsome jewelry in this book. At the upper right, with red handles, is a pair of round-nose pliers and, with black handles, a pair of plate shears.

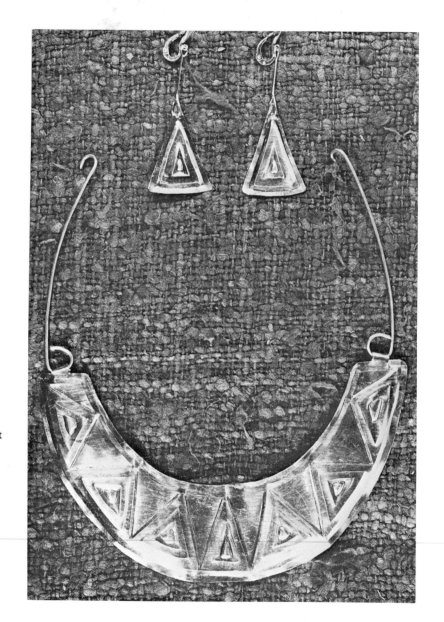

Illus. 33. A unique gorget and earrings made from silver sheet.

Silver Gorget and Matching Earrings

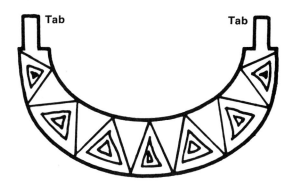

Illus. 34. Be sure to make tabs on each end for attaching the round wire.

Materials
26-gauge sheet silver
16-gauge, or heavier, round wire
24-gauge, or lighter, round wire
earring findings
scissors
paper and grease pencil
pliers and knitting needle
bone folder and embossing mat

Here you can achieve a medieval look by fashioning a silver gorget, originally a crescent-shaped piece of armor worn to protect the throat, beginning in the 15th century.

Make a paper pattern of the sheet silver crescent and measure it (using string for the wire pieces) around your neck. Allow for two tabs on each end.

Sketch your design on the paper. Notice the variance in shape and size of the triangles used in Illus. 33. You need not use this design, however,

but keep it simple since this is a fairly large piece of silver and you won't want to spoil it.

Transfer your outline in grease pencil to the silver, as well as the design. Cut, not forgetting the tabs. Work lightly and carefully on your embossing with the bone folder, being sure to use the mat.

Form the wire pieces from the heavy round wire after measuring with string and the paper pattern. The two tabs will form the attachment, so do not tightly close the bottom wire loops yet.

Roll the tabs toward the back using a knitting needle until you have formed cylinders of a size that will accommodate the wire. Slip the wires through and squeeze tight.

Make matching earrings as shown (also using paper patterns) and hook onto ready-made findings of either the ear clip or screwback type in the style called "pierced look." These have tiny hooks at the base for attaching dangles.

Illus. 36. An unusual idea—an ear clip! Use a clip-on earring finding. You will find many ways of using this simple adornment—how about a shoe buckle?

Illus. 35 (opposite page). To make this stunning hairclasp or brooch of hammered silver sheet and wire, see page 30 for basic procedures.

A Personalized Silver and Bead Barrette

Illus. 37.

Materials

18- or 20-gauge sheet silver
26-gauge round wire
large, bulbous bead
barrette finding, ready-made
plate shears
round-nose pliers
tweezers
heavy needle
epoxy cement
bone folder and embossing mat

Make a paper pattern of your chosen monogram. Since a barrette receives a certain amount of bending and pressure, do not use very thin sheet silver. Although 18 gauge is most often used for such things as money clips and tie clips, you can use, if necessary, 22 gauge. Use plate shears for cutting out your transferred pattern.

Keep your embossing as simple as possible since you will find you must work heavier silver more times on each side.

Cement the bead on and create an "artificial bezel" by piercing a hole alongside it and drawing a length of 26-gauge wire through. Wrap this around the bead as many times as you can, but don't bury the bead! Do this by holding about $\frac{1}{2}''$ of wire at the back with the pliers and use a tweezer for wrapping. (A good idea to prevent marring is to cover the tweezer ends with adhesive tape.) Make a few twists at the back to secure it and snip off the excess.

Cement the finished barrette to a ready-made finding.

Spiralled Flat-Wire Belt and Armband

Materials
    18-gauge silver flat wire
    round-nose and flat-nose pliers
    string
    tape measure
Both the belt and the armband are made from just two pieces of flat wire.

The length of the belt will depend upon how you are going to wear it—around your waist or on your hips. Use the string method for measuring, and allow at least 5″ on each end for spiralling. After spiralling, twist the wire just in back of the spirals 90° (Illus. 22) upward. In Illus. 38, these are the small spirals on top.

The two large spirals which appear to disappear into the small spirals are actually made from one piece and looped *over* the small spirals on the end of the belt, serving as a clasp. After cutting approximately a 10″ length of flat wire, make the two spirals and then cross them over each other using the pliers. You will find that to make them lie flat in relationship to each other you must make a 45° twist in each.

The armband, or slip-on bracelet, does not have

Illus. 38.

a clasp, so allow for being able to get it over your hand. (Use string to measure.)

First make the back part of the bracelet, bending into a large semi-circle a length of wire with a small spiral on either end. Again, allow 5″ for these spirals.

Then take a longer piece of flat wire which should be equal to the remaining semi-circle, plus about 10″. Thread this through each spiral and bring the long ends toward you. Wind larger spirals on each end. Then bend the whole thing back toward the other part till the two spirals meet. Give each a 90° twist upwards, so they are in the position illustrated.

A Beaded Wire Necklace and Bracelet

Materials
- 12-gauge silver round wire
- 18-gauge silver flat wire
- quantity of beads with large eyes
- mallet and anvil
- round-nose pliers

Fashion a choker-type neckloop from the 12-gauge round wire, leaving the ends free for threading. Cut the flat wire into about forty 2″ lengths. (Don't worry if you cut too many—you will use them in the bracelet.) One by one, flatten them out in a tapering fashion so that one end is wider than the other. Form closed loops at one end large enough to accommodate the 12-gauge wire easily.

Then bend each piece around the round-nose pliers so that there is a single spiral-like turn as shown in Illus. 39. Now start stringing alternately the wire and the beads, beginning and ending with a wire. Leave a length of at least 3″ free on each end of the 12-gauge wire.

You can vary the pattern any way you wish, of course. You might prefer two beads, then one silver piece, or vice versa. Experiment until you like the appearance of it. Then make the clasp shown in Illus. 40, using the ends of the 12-gauge wire.

Make the bracelet in exactly the same way, or as we did using two pieces of 12-gauge wire to form a double width. In this case, do not taper the silver pieces—instead, form a closed loop at each end and proceed to thread. You will then need to make a double clasp as well.

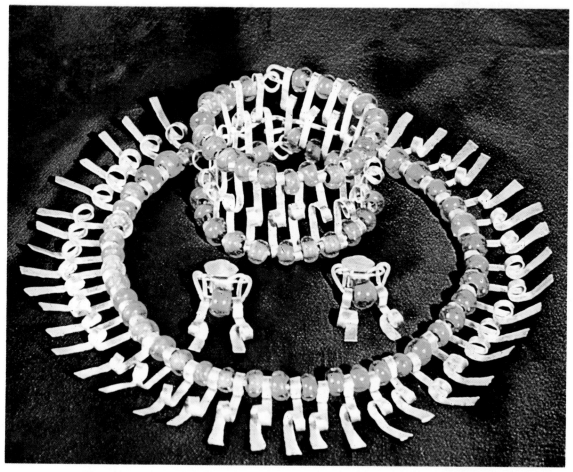

Illus. 39. As ornate as this lovely set looks, it is as easy as your first project.

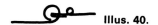 Illus. 40.

Illus. 41. Use paper patterns for embossing (page 14) this silver bangle necklace and earrings. Assemble with 24-gauge hammered wire loops (Illus. 19).

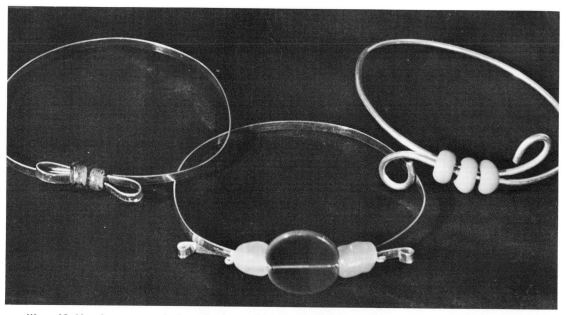

Illus. 42. You have your choice of wire and beads in these charming, easy-to-make bracelets.

Illus. 43. This monogrammed adornment on a leather handbag is made in the same fashion as the barrette on page 30.

Illus. 44. A metal frame available at hobby shops is the base for this gaily festooned lamp shade.

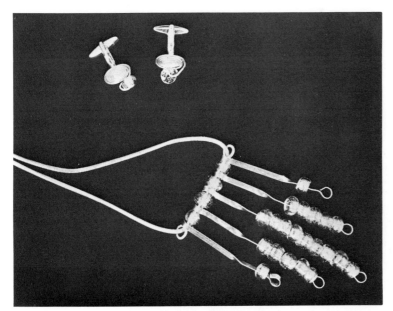

Neckpiece and

Cuff Links

Illus. 45.

Materials

28-gauge silver round wire

22-gauge silver round wire

18-gauge silver flat wire

large, large-eyed beads (preferably wooden)

leather thong (available at hobby and shoe repair shops)

cuff-link findings

mallet and anvil

epoxy cement

To make the neckpiece, string four beads on a 3″ piece of 22-gauge round wire. Form closed loops on each end. Cut five pieces of the flat wire

in three different lengths as shown. Twist each 90° with the pliers at different points—the shortest pieces, twist closer to the ends. String beads on as far as each twist will allow. Make closing loops on the ends. Then attach the assembly between the beads on the round wire with simple hooked-over ends. Pass a leather thong through the upper piece and merely tie it in back when you wear it.

Next, wind two pieces of 28-gauge wire into spirals, leaving about an 1″ free on one end of each. Hammer them almost flat. Slip a bead on each, and twist the ends slightly back to hold them on. Glue the flattened spirals onto the cuff-link findings with epoxy cement.

37

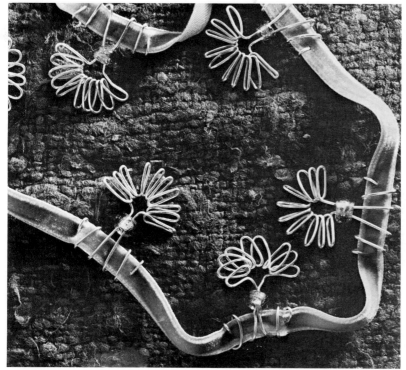

Wire-and-Bead-Decorated Belt

Illus. 46.

Materials
   22-gauge round wire
   beads
   heavy velvet ribbon
   flat-nose pliers

Here is an elegant belt to wear on special occasions. The design easily can be adapted to matching accessories—bracelet, necklace, earrings. You are going to make a different kind of spiral now which you will also use in later projects.

Wrap a length of wire around a cylindrical

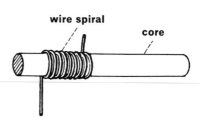

Illus. 47.

38

object as shown in Illus. 47, at least ten times, leaving $2\frac{1}{2}''$ of straight wire on both ends. Remove, and with the flat-nose pliers, squeeze the coil until it assumes an elongated shape. Then pull the loops apart so that they fan out as shown. Press the two straight ends together, thread on a bead, and then form the ends into two "belt loops."

Make at least a dozen of these ornaments and slip on the velvet band. A simple bow or knot serves as an appropriate clasp.

Hammered Silver Round-Wire Hairpin

Materials
    20-gauge silver round wire
    26-gauge silver round wire
    medium-large flat brooch with pinback
    mallet and anvil
    plate shears
    flat-nose pliers
    knitting needle
    epoxy cement

Shape a 9″ length of 20-gauge wire into an ordinary hairpin shape as shown. With your mallet, carefully flatten it out on the anvil. Then, with the flat-nose pliers, bend the loop at the top over a knitting needle to the shape shown in Illus. 48.

Most pinback findings have a loop and ring arrangement of some kind on each end. Close over the loop end and through the resulting two rings, slip the hairpin and work it up to within $1\frac{1}{2}''$ of the top.

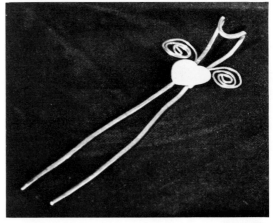

Illus. 48.

Make two little hammered spirals and cement the end of each onto the back of the brooch. Bend the long ends of the hairpin outward into a slightly bowed shape to provide tension for the brooch portion. Snip off ends if too long.

39

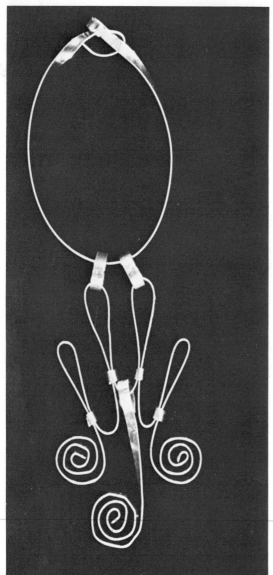

A Flat-Wire Key Ring

Materials
   narrow silver flat wire
   flat-nose pliers
   round-nose pliers
   scissors

Here is a key ring you will never find in any shop in the world! Make an oval loop about 3″ in length with the flat wire. Give each end a 90° twist and form loops that will hook onto each other as a clasp. These twists will prevent keys from slipping off easily.

With one piece of flat wire about 12″ long, form a loose spiral on each end. Then bend carefully into the four elongated loops as shown. Cut four 1″ lengths of wire and wrap around each loop as shown to form secure clips.

Make a third spiralled piece and suspend it from the middle of the main part. Attach the assembly onto the large loop with two flat-wire round rings.

Illus. 49.

40

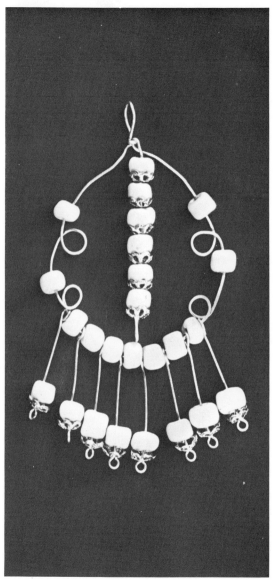

Round-Wire-and-Bead

Key Ring Pendant

Materials
    28-gauge round wire
    quantity of small beads
    bead cups (available at hobby and craft supply
      shops)
    round-nose pliers
    plate shears

If you want to add a new look to an old key ring that you don't want to part with, here is the answer.

Form the main oval loop by first making the four small loops with the wire laid out straight. Thread the beads on as you go. Then bend the entire thing into a loop shape. Make a clasp at the ends as in Illus. 10.

Now string beads and bead cups onto a piece of round wire and attach at the clasp and the base of the main section as shown. Bead cups almost always have a small ring at the underside of the base, so *beforehand,* using your plate shears, snip these off so there is a small hole in each through which to string the wire.

The hanging pieces are all made from equal-length pieces of wire with a single bead and cup strung on and attached to the main section with tiny loops.

Illus. 50.

Spiralled Round-Wire Bottle Collar

Materials
  20-gauge silver round wire
  28-gauge silver round wire
  small glass beads
  velvet ribbon
  round-nose pliers
  pencil

Make the large springlike part by winding the 20-gauge wire tightly around a pencil. Do the same with the inner springy part but pull out as shown. Twist all the ends together and attach to the ribbon.

The decorative hanging pieces are made with the 28-gauge wire. Take one piece, bend in two and twist carefully with your hands so that you create a "rope," or chain effect. Leave about $2\frac{1}{2}''$ on each end and make spirals. Now, with the pliers, pull out the inner ends of these spirals and form tiny eyeletlike loops.

Cut two pieces of 28-gauge wire about 3" long. Thread one through each eyelet, place a bead on each end and form closing loops.

Cut two more pieces 2" long and thread one through the closing loops on the top of each beaded part. Make closing loops again. Then, do the same with the other piece, attaching it to the bottom closing loops of the beaded parts. These

Illus. 51.

two horizontal pieces will serve to hold the beaded parts stiff.

Attach the upper end of the twisted, ropelike part to the velvet ribbon also. Make two identical decorative pieces to hang on the sides, or vary as you wish.

A Round-Wire Wall Decoration

Materials
   20-gauge silver round wire
   18-gauge silver flat wire
   beads
   brooch
   bead cups
   epoxy cement

You can make this lovely ornament any size you wish. Using the same method for the belt you made on page 38, wind the round wire round a cylinder. Slip a length of flat wire through the resulting spiral and form into a long oval. Make a 90° twist on each flat-wire end.

Form the middle piece by shaping a circle the appropriate size to accommodate the brooch. Then form a twisted end, slip a bead and cup on, and attach where the spiralled ends meet. Glue the brooch onto the circular portion.

Make the pendant parts exactly as you did on page 41. This piece can be used in many ways—on a Christmas tree, a mirror, in a window, or, even in a car window!

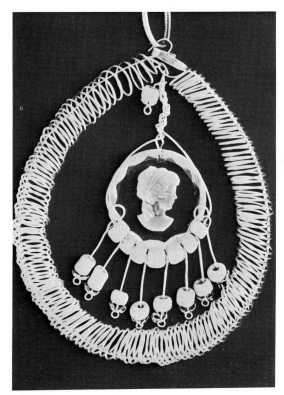

Illus. 52.

43

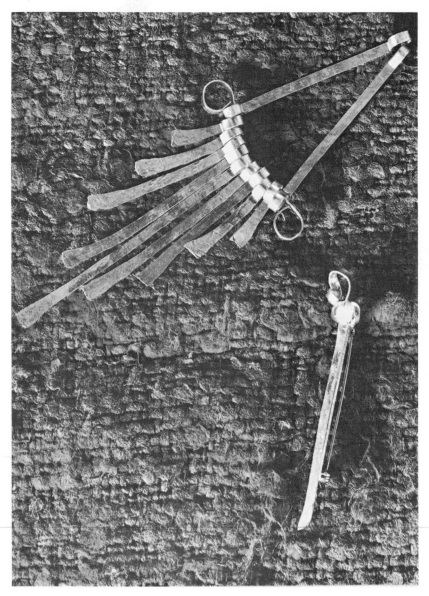

Illus. 53. A neck pendant and cravat pin are easily fashioned from hammered flat wire. A pinback finding is glued to the back of the cravat pin.

44

Illus. 54. A single piece of flat wire with spiralled ends forms each of these earrings. Tiny spirals are attached to the findings as "cover-ups."

Illus. 55. A scarf pin of twisted and spiralled flat wire is attached to a pinback finding. The rings are made in the same way as the bracelets in Illus. 42.

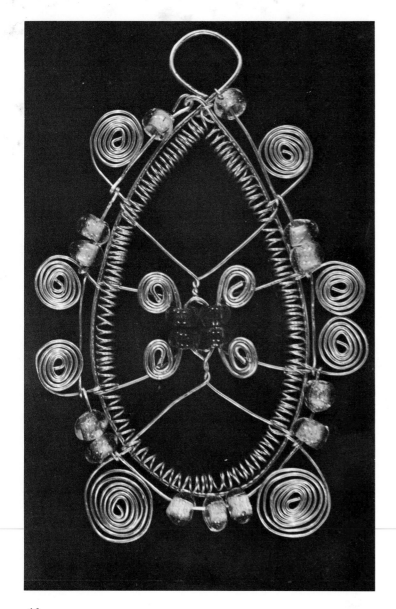

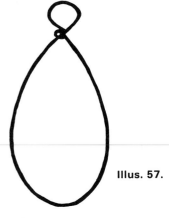

Illus. 56. This lovely Christmas decoration can be adapted to many uses. It is made of seven separate pieces joined together.

Illus. 57.

A Wire-and-Bead Christmas Decoration

Materials

   18-gauge round wire
   22-gauge round wire
   large-eyed beads
   knitting needle
   round-nose pliers

Shape a long oval loop with the 18-gauge wire in the size that you desire. Make a clasp as in Illus. 10.

Next, make the two spiral pieces in the middle, each with two beads. (Be sure to use large-eyed beads because they will have to accommodate three pieces of wire.) Then take a length of wire and thread it through one pair of these beads, bend the ends and wrap them around the 18-gauge wire loop once. Make spirals with the remaining ends. Do the same with the other spiral and bead part. You should now have something that looks like this:

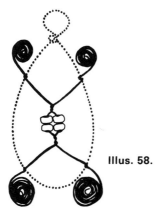

Illus. 58.

Now take two more wires, pass one through each set of beads, and twist them a couple of times just above and below the beads. Attach the four ends as shown to the 18-gauge loop in the same way as before—wrap once around it and make spirals on the ends.

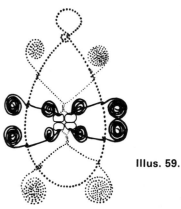

Illus. 59.

Then wrap 22-gauge wire around a knitting needle to form the large coiled part. Separate the loops a little by pulling on the ends of the wire. Bend into a long oval and rest it on the eight wire supports you just made so that it fits snugly within the 18-gauge loop. Hook onto the loop at the top.

The final step is to take a long piece of 22-gauge wire. Hook one end onto the clasp of the 18-gauge loop. Thread on a bead, wrap the wire once around the first spiral going counterclockwise. Slip on two beads and go on to the next spiral. Continue in this manner until you come back to the beginning, and you'll have a beautiful and unique Christmas ornament.

47

Index

angled forms, 7, 17
anvil, 7
armband, 31
attachment loops, 16

barrette, 30
bead cups, 41, 43
beads, 6
belts, 21, 31, 38
bending, 6
bending aids, 7, 11, 14, 17
bezels, artificial, 30
bone folder, 7
bottle collar, 42
bracelets, 8, 11, 31, 32, 33, 35
brooch, 28

cameos, 15, 16
chokers, 22, 23
Christmas decoration, 47
clasps, 6, 10, 11, 13
cravat pin, 44
cuff links, 37
cutting, 7

diagonal-cutting pliers, 7

ear adornment, 29
earrings, 12, 13, 26, 27, 34
embossing, 4, 7, 14, 27, 30
epoxy cement, 7
epoxy-cement remover, 12

findings, 7, 27
flat-nose pliers, 6, 7
flattening wire, 5, 7, 16
flat wire, 5, 6

gauges, 5, 6
glueing, 7
gorget, 26, 27

hairclasp, 28
hairpin, 39
hammering, 5, 7, 16, 39

jump rings, 12, 13

key rings, 40, 41

lamp shade, 36
links, 16, 21

mallets, 7
materials, 5–6, 25
mats, embossing, 14
measurements, 9
metal-cutting shears, 7, 25
modelling tool, 14

necklaces, 8, 9, 12, 13, 14, 15, 17,
   19, 20, 32, 34, 37

paper patterns, 12, 24, 27

pendants, 12, 13, 14, 15, 16, 17,
   19, 20, 41, 46
plate shears, 7, 25
pliers, diagonal-cutting, 7
pliers, flat-nose, 6, 7
pliers, round-nose, 6, 25

rings, 45
rounded forms, 6, 11
round-nose pliers, 6, 25
round wire, 5, 6

scarf pin, 45
scissors, 7
shears, metal-cutting, 7, 25
shears, plate, 7, 25
sheet silver, 5, 6
spiralling, 18, 38
spirals, 15, 17
squeezing, 7
string measurements, 9

tabs, 27
thongs, 37
"threading," 9, 10, 11
tools, 6–7
tweezers, 30
twisting, 18, 30

wall decoration, 43
wire, 5–6